Kristaps Porzingis

A Biography of the Latvian Superstar

BENJAMIN SOUTHERLAND

Table of Contents

Chapter 1: Latvia, Basketball and Family

There is nowhere in sports where a player is under the microscope, in the spotlight and constantly critiqued like New York City. It is the media capital of the world, and there is a huge focus on the New York Knicks who play in "The World's Most Famous Arena," Madison Square Garden. It takes a special type of athlete to survive in that environment, let alone thrive or become a superstar and fan favorite. Kristaps Porzingis did all of that, instantly becoming one of the Big Apple's biggest sporting attractions.

New Yorkers didn't take to Porzingis immediately, when the Knicks drafted him there was no unanimous applause and a standing ovation. But what they, and NBA fans all around the world, didn't know was that Porzingis had been planning, learning and practicing all his life for the chance to be a superstar for the Knicks. When he got his chance, he was more than ready for it. Nearly as many people live in the New York City borough of Manhattan as do live in Latvia. It has been an amazing journey for Kristaps Porzingis from the small city of Liepaja, Latvia to the starting lineup of the New York Knicks.

He was born on August 2, 1995. In the NBA, the Houston Rockets were the champions. Expansion teams Toronto and Vancouver arrived. Don Nelson had just been hired to coach the Knicks. Pat Riley had gone to the Heat to coach and do everything else there. Danny Ainge and Bill Cartwright retired after long playing careers. Dennis Rodman would be traded to the Bulls around that time and three more championships would then arrive in Chicago. Nobody in the NBA knew that the future of the sport had entered the world and it was a Latvian.

Kristaps did have several advantages, due to genetics and all the experience in basketball his family had to share with him. His mother, Ingrida Porzingis, was a 6-1 player for the Latvian national team at youth level. His father, Talis Porzingis, was a 6-4 player in the days of the U.S.S.R. but wasn't a star player and didn't appear in any high-profile competitions. His older brothers played basketball in Europe, and importantly played against their baby brother and helped him improve.

His oldest brother is Janis Porzingis, who was born in 1982 and is 13 years older than Kristaps. A 6-8 small forward, Janis played professionally in Latvia, Lithuania,

Austria, Sweden, Belgium, Hungary, Italy, Spain and Croatia. The high point of his playing career was joining Basket Livorno and playing in the top Italian league. Martins Porzingis is 6-4 in height, and Kristaps' other brother also played professional basketball.

Just as ice hockey legend Wayne Gretzky had the advantage of growing up with a hockey rink in his backyard built by his father, Kristaps Porzingis was able to play basketball whenever he wanted because his father and the family built a court in his backyard. It was a wooden outdoor court, with a chain net on the basket. He learned the game there, and tried to play like his NBA heroes.

He was 6 years old when his mother took him to a local gym so he could join a basketball team. Many skillful NBA players started as point guards when they were children. Scottie Pippen and Kelly Olynyk played there, before they grew to forward and center size, while a young Porzingis played the point even though he was the tallest player on his youth team. It allowed Porzingis to develop his skills as he had the ball in his hands more. The biggest basketball club in his hometown was BK Liepajas Lauvas. Porzingis would play for their youth team. He played there until he was 15.

While a young Kristaps played basketball wherever and whenever he could, some of the best games were in his own backyard. It was Kristaps and Janis against Martins and their father, Talis. Martins would use physical defense on Kristaps, emulating the way Latvian power forward Kaspars Kambala played. His brothers were training Kristaps to be a star in Europe, as it wasn't until he was 17 years old that his brothers really thought he had NBA potential.

The city of Liepaja is in the west of Latvia, on the coast of the Baltic Sea. Around 80,000 people live there, and nobody as famous as Porzingis has come from there. Nobody as world famous as Porzingis has come from the entire country of Latvia. Before Porzingis, NHL goalie Arturs Irbe may have been the Latvian with the greatest profile. He played 568 games in the National Hockey League. Zemgus Girgensons is a more recent Latvian star in the NHL; he scored 15 goals for Buffalo in the 2014-15 season. Kristaps Porzingis never wanted to be a hockey player, and he looked up to basketball players as role models.

While he had plenty of people to admire in his family, Kristaps Porzingis also found basketball heroes elsewhere, players from Latvia and also the NBA. There is a famous picture of a young Kristaps with a hairstyle that was not common to Latvia, and one that was influenced by Carmelo Anthony and Allen Iverson. Porzingis as a child with cornrows, made him stand out in Latvia at the time, and it would also be something useful for him to talk about to a new teammate years later when he joined the Knicks.

Other NBA players influenced him over the years. Kevin Garnett was a player he and his brothers watched. He was a good player for Porzingis to study, as he was a similar NBA player, very long and very skilled. German Dirk Nowitzki also got his attention, and Porzingis hoped to be able to do Dirk's one-foot, step-back shot. Later he would also have Anthony Davis as one of his favorite players too. He has mentioned Kobe Bryant, and how he studied how Kobe and Michael Jordan acted during interviews, and also that he had a Carmelo Anthony jersey.

Martins talked about what he was pointing out to Kristaps when they watched NBA players off the court. It was about "how to answer questions, when to smile, when not to smile, stuff like that. It sounds a little weird, but you have to prepare for that if you go to the NBA." Kristaps entire family helped him on his way to the NBA, in ways that as a 14 year old watching a video of NBA players talking he would not have known.

Something that Porzingis didn't have that so many other young players around the world had was NBA games on television when he was awake. Due to the time zone differences, if someone in Latvia wants to watch the NBA they have to stay up all night or set the alarm clock to wake up very, very early. With Porzingis now in the NBA, many more Latvians watch games. That wasn't the case when Porzingis was a child there. Kristaps Porzingis has said that "getting up early in the morning to watch the Lakers" is something he remembers as an early NBA moment for him during his childhood.

If Kristaps wanted to try to emulate Pau Gasol and Kobe Bryant in the NBA it meant moving away from his family and Latvia, at a young age. He had a big choice to make, a short distance to the east, a long move across the Atlantic, or somewhere much warmer in Europe where basketball was big.

Chapter 2: Moving to Spain to Improve His Game

With the NBA being Porzingis' main goal, he needed to set on a path to that destination, and that probably required leaving Latvia. He needed a country with a bigger basketball league, with better players, one that would challenge him and improve his game. He did have several options, in Europe and overseas.

The traditional path to the NBA is an American high school followed by an American college. Many European, and other international, prospects have found their way to the NBA by doing that. Others skip the high school part, but go to college for the greatest exposure there is to NBA scouts. Another Latvian player had got close to the NBA after graduating from an American high school and then college, Kaspars Kambala.

Kambala was the most famous basketball name in Latvia when Porzingis was growing up there. He went from

Latvia to Homestead High School in Mequon, Wisconsin. Kambala then enrolled at UNLV, the University of Nevada, Las Vegas. Kambala battled in the paint for four seasons, and as a senior he averaged 17 points and 9 rebounds. He was surprisingly undrafted, and although he was invited to the Summer League he never got to the NBA. Porzingis could look to Detlef Schrempf as a success story, he left what was then West Germany for high school and college in America and it took him to a long NBA career.

Instead of following the path of Kambala, Porzingis decided to do what his brothers did and look to Europe. Janis Porzingis may have had his greatest success in Italy, while also playing in several other countries. He had a brief stop in Spain, playing for Palencia Baloncesto, and Porzingis chose that country to move to.

From Latvia, there is nearly nowhere further away on the continent than Spain, but there was also no basketball league that was considered to be as good as the Spanish league. It would end up being the right choice by Porzingis, and it wasn't too far for the rest of his family, as they would all jump in a bus and drive all the way to Spain to see him play. Kristaps' other plan was to stay in Latvia, move to the bigger city of Riga and play for VEF Riga. That team does now have a connection to the New York Knicks as former Knick Josh Harrellson signed with the team for the 2015-16 season.

Kristaps Porzingis signed with Sevilla. An agent in Latvia had contacted various teams around Europe and Sevilla was one that showed interest. They invited Porzingis to Spain for a tryout, and a potential spot on their youth team.

Spain to the NBA was a path that had worked for European prospects. Pau Gasol, someone with a similar build and game to Porzingis, was a huge NBA success with multiple NBA championships and honors. The summer of 2010 was when Porzingis signed with Sevilla. A year before, Ricky Rubio made headlines by being drafted in the top five of the NBA draft after several seasons playing in the Spanish league.

"I came here with my brother for two or three days, but it was really hot and I couldn't play at my best because of that." That was how Porzingis described his tryout with Sevilla. But the team was not worried about that, as they had a chance to sign a 15 year old that was 6-8 in height and a great athlete, and was expected to grow to a much larger height.

Plenty of superstar basketball players had a roadblock to the NBA, and after going to one team in their youth decided it wasn't for them. Larry Bird signed with prestigious Indiana University but quickly decided it wasn't for him and went back home. Kristaps Porzingis was teetering on leaving Spain very early in his time there. It was certainly different to his native country and there were other circumstances that were pushing him back home.

"The first half of my first season was really tough for me. I didn't know any Spanish and only a few people spoke English. I had trouble to communicate with my teammates and coaches. Moreover, I had anemia so I didn't last long in practices. I didn't feel good and was sleepy all the time." Going from Latvian food to a Spanish diet was an adjustment that was difficult for him. It also took several months for the problem to be found that was causing his tiredness; anemia.

Porzingis was 6-9 and 160 pounds, rail thin, and also suffering from a decrease in red blood cells. Due to that, his muscles were getting less oxygen. He was getting tired very quickly. Changes to diet and iron pills got the situation under control and Porzingis could focus on basketball now that his body was right. He would play five games for the Sevilla junior team in season 2011-12. The next season he played more junior team games, but after 24 points and 11 rebounds against Real Madrid's youth team it was time for Kristaps to play in the big league.

Porzingis would play 10 games for Cajasol Sevilla in 2012-13. The team was led on the floor by Tomas Satoransky, a tall guard who had been drafted by the

Washington Wizards, but would stay in Europe. Porzingis played for a few minutes, and his Liga ACB and Eurocup season averages were 2 points and 1 rebound in 6.6 minutes per game. He shot 50% from the field.

Porzingis made a big impact for his country at the U18 European Championship in 2013. He made the All Tournament Team along with Anzejs Pasecniks, Paolo Marinelli, Domagoj Bosnjak and tournament MVP Kenan Sipahi. Porzingis brought defense, with 5 blocks and 10 rebounds per game. In the last game Latvia played in the tournament he had 11 points, 15 rebounds and 9 blocks.

For season 2013-14 with Sevilla, Porzingis played next to a former Knick, forward Marcus Landry. Porzingis appeared in 32 Spanish league games. He had around 7 points, 5 rebounds and a block per game. He played around 15 minutes a game. For his draft prospects, his per 36 minutes statistics looked very promising. They were 16.2 points, 6.6 rebounds, 2.3 blocks, 1.4 steals and 1.2 three-pointers made. His free throw and three-point percentages were not great, but his field goal number of 47.6% was a solid number.

Doing well against the biggest teams in a league is important, for a draft prospect, as that is often where the scouts are. Against Real Madrid on April 6, 2014,

Porzingis hit 8 of 12 shots from the field and scored 20 points. Earlier in the season he had 13 points, on 5 of 8 shooting, against Real Madrid. There were now NBA teams ready to draft him in the first round.

Chapter 3: Declaring for the 2014 NBA Draft

The Porzingis Era of the NBA nearly started one year earlier. He declared for the 2014 NBA Draft and there were teams ready to guarantee him a spot in the first round. If he had stayed in the draft, his career and the entire NBA could have been very different. Imagine Porzingis at power forward for the Orlando Magic or as the 6th Man for the Oklahoma City Thunder, it nearly happened.

Porzingis had his name in the 2014 draft for two months. In late April 2014 he declared for the NBA draft; but he disappointed some teams, and basketball fans, when his name was on the list of early entrants that were withdrawing, released by the NBA on June 17. His withdrawal was the only one that created a stir, as few had heard of players like Devon Van Oostrum, Alejandro Suarez and Eleftherios Bochoridis who also had also taken their names out of the draft.

While a lot of NBA teams are talked about after drafts and how they really would have liked to pick a certain prospect, there was news in June of 2014 that the Thunder had made a promise to select Kristaps if he remained in the draft. A report on ESPN in early June said, "A few weeks ago it seemed unlikely that Porzingis would keep his name in the draft. The 18-year-old Latvian was projected as a potential top-10 pick next year. But sources now say Porzingis has received a promise from the Thunder to draft him in the first round."

The Thunder had drafted well, and were a contender. Their picks in recent drafts included Kevin Durant, Russell Westbrook, Serge Ibaka, James Harden, Reggie Jackson and Steven Adams. Ibaka was drafted by the franchise while he was playing in Spain. If they had landed Porzingis it might have pushed them to the championship, but they didn't get the chance as he didn't stay in the draft. The OKC Thunder would eventually use pick number 21 on power forward Mitch McGary.

After Porzingis became an instant phenomenon during his first NBA season, many more stories came out for which teams had been hoping to grab him in 2014. At the top of the list, according to Yahoo!, was the Orlando Magic. They had pick number 12, as well as a deal agreed to which moved them up to pick 10, so it is very likely he would not have found his way to the Thunder later in the first round.

For the Magic, Porzingis would have been the perfect fit. They needed a power forward, the Magic also needed height for their roster and shooting, Kristaps was everything they needed. The new Magic frontline would have been Porzingis at power forward next to center Nikola Vucevic and small forward Tobias Harris. With Victor Oladipo and Evan Fournier at the guard spots it would have been a young, athletic and exciting team.

The Magic would actually pick a power forward with the fourth overall pick, Aaron Gordon, and later in the lottery they moved up from pick number 12 to pick number 10 to select point guard Elfrid Payton. The 2014 NBA Draft was considered to be a three player draft, as the top three prospects Andrew Wiggins, Jabari Parker and Joel Embiid were ranked as much better players than any others available in the draft, and if workouts or pre-draft hype had Porzingis moving up draft boards the Magic may have had to grab him with pick number 4 as plenty of other teams were willing to roll the dice.

A report from ESPN in early June mentioned that there were several teams who were becoming more impressed with Porzingis the more they watched and researched him. As well as the Magic and Thunder, the Boston Celtics and Atlanta Hawks were said to be possible destinations in the 2014 draft. The Celtics had two picks in the first round, 6 and 17, while the Hawks were getting ready to make a choice at number 15. Boston would pick guards Marcus Smart and James Young, although it was said they wanted Aaron Gordon but he didn't last to their first pick. The Hawks obviously wanted a player like Porzingis as their choice was a power forward who had range on his shooting and could also block shots, Adreian Payne from Michigan State.

An unnamed general manager was on the money when he talked to ESPN about Porzingis after he removed his name from the draft, "He's very talented. He wasn't ready, but we would've seriously considered drafting him anyway. If he continues to develop his game, get more minutes and his body develops, I think he could be a top-five pick in 2015. He has that kind of talent." He certainly did become a top-five pick a year later.

Porzingis did go to the U.S.A. at that time to show teams what he could do after declaring for the draft. Not all of it went to plan; when he arrived it was without his luggage, which had been misplaced by the airline. "Vegas is actually the first city I went to when I came to the U.S. last summer, when I trained at Impact Basketball gym with Joe Abunassar. My first night in Vegas, after my airline baggage got lost, I had my first filet mignon at Caesars Palace, and it's now one of my favorite foods because it's healthy."

Declaring for the draft helped Porzingis because NBA teams were not sure if a superstar could come from

Latvia, and the publicity that Porzingis got from declaring in 2014 made sure that more NBA teams scouted him more closely in the following twelve months. Prior to Porzingis, only two players born in Latvia had taken the court in the National Basketball Association.

The first Latvian NBA player was Gundars Vetra. Maybe he is the answer to a difficult trivia question, very few people knew he even played in the NBA. He had 89 minutes of playing time in 1992-93 with the Minnesota Timberwolves. A 6-6 swingman, Vetra shot a solid 47.5% from the field for 3.5 points per game. He would play, and later coach, for many seasons in Europe. Vetra didn't exactly pave the way for Latvians to enter the NBA, but the next Latvian did help Porzingis by being a lottery pick.

Andris Biedrins spent a decade in the NBA. From the Latvian capital city of Riga, Biedrins not only put Latvian basketball on the map by entering the NBA as the 11th pick in 2004 but he also led the league in a statistical category. In 2007-08 he led the NBA in field goal percentage with 62.6%. He was long like Porzingis, 6-11 in height, but stronger and he started 311 of his 516 games he played for Golden State. Andris may have helped teams see that Latvia could produce NBA players, which was good for Porzingis, and he also helped the Warriors land an important championship piece when

Golden State sent him and other players, plus draft picks, to clear salary and land free agent Andre Iguodala.

Putting his name in the draft was a good move. During the 2014-15 season in Spain NBA scouts and general managers took many trips to his games in Spain. He had the eyes of the NBA on him and all he had to do was show he deserved to be a lottery pick by playing well. He may have exceeded the expectations of his fans in Spain and NBA teams.

Chapter 4: Season 2014-15 in Spain with Sevilla

There would be no great team success as Porzingis spent another season in Spain, but his draft stock was greatly enhanced by the numbers he put up. Sevilla had 19 wins and 31 losses. Porzingis increased his scoring and rebounding rate, and importantly showed the NBA his shooting touch was even better as his free throw numbers took an important leap forward.

Porzingis played 34 Liga ACB games in 2014-15 with Sevilla plus another 16 in the Eurocup. His Spanish league numbers were 21.7 minutes, 10.7 points, 4.8 rebounds, 1 block and 0.9 steals per game. His per minute numbers increased for points and rebounds, compared to his previous season, while he fouled at a much lower rate. His percentages were more important to his draft stock. While his field goal and three-point numbers didn't change a lot, his free throw number in Spanish league play went from 60.7% to 77.4%. That showed everyone in the NBA that Porzingis was a rare combination of height, athleticism and skill.

Against Basquet Manresa, Porzingis had a game that showed how he could dominate and get his team the win by getting to the free throw line. He shot 10 free throws, hitting 9. He finished the game with 19 points, 7 rebounds, 1 steal and 1 block.

A game against CAI Zaragoza showed Porzingis' defensive abilities. In 21 minutes he had 4 blocks and 1 steal. He didn't neglect the offensive end of the court, he hit 2 of 5 threes and went 4 of 8 from the field to finish with 10 points.

While Porzingis was playing well in Europe, his competition for the top spot in the 2015 NBA Draft was putting up numbers in the NCAA. Jahlil Okafor helped Duke to a national championship and for the season averaged 17.3 points and 8.5 rebounds. Karl-Anthony Towns showed great improvement during the season at Kentucky. To get them into the Final 4, he shot 10 of 13 from the field for 25 points against Notre Dame. His season averages were 10.3 points and 6.7 rebounds in 21.1 minutes, while he shot really well with 56.6% from the field and 81.3% on free throws.

Highlight plays from Porzingis were something fans came to expect in his NBA rookie season and in Spain in

2014-15 they happened a lot too. In a game against Real Madrid, he caught the ball at the three-point line and waited as a defender ran at him, he then put the ball on the floor and drove to the basket to dunk over another defender. Against Barcelona and their roster of talented players, he helped get Sevilla the win and put on a show for the many scouts in the crowd. A highlight was catching a lob for a giant dunk. He just missed a two-handed putback slam.

NBA scouts were sending reports back to their teams, sometimes saying they recommended Porzingis as the top overall pick, and he was also impressing veterans on his team. Derrick Byers was his teammate that season, a 6-7 forward who played all over the world and briefly for the San Antonio Spurs. He said, "I was very impressed with him. His skillset is what impressed me the most, but there was another thing, toughness. Here was a 19-year-old player playing with grown men with that skinny frame, but you could tell he was mentally tough. He had confidence."

Willy Hernangomez, another Sevilla teammate and one who was on a path to the Knicks too, saw how Porzingis was preparing himself for the NBA in 2013-14 more than he had the previous year. "When he had American players, he would always try to engage with them to learn things about the States, to improve his English, ask for advice for the future. Especially his final year in Seville, you could tell he was thinking about this big chance of making it to the NBA."

If Porzingis thought he needed to show NBA scouts that he was the best draft prospect in Europe, he did it by winning the 2014-15 Eurocup Rising Star Trophy. He was 19 years old, and won an award that was also open to older players, as the rule was to be eligible a player needed to be less than 22 when the season started.

His Eurocup statistics were 11.6 points, 4.1 rebounds and 1.2 blocks per game. Porzingis shot 45.9% on three-pointers. As he played around 20 minutes a game, those who scouted his games could see that if he were playing a lot more his numbers would be close to a superstar level. It also helped Porzingis that past winners included Donatas Motiejunas and Jonas Valanciunas, two players whose skills had directly translated to the NBA, which showed that a young European prospect like Porzingis could find success in the NBA.

There wasn't anything that Porzingis couldn't do on the court. He could run around screens like a guard, catch the ball and hit the three-pointer. He could establish position inside, and then turn and score off the backboard. Shooting, passing, defending, he had learned how to do it all.

His time in Spain had been everything he hoped it would be. He arrived as a thin and very young project player, and he left as an NBA-ready player who was fluent in three languages and did things on the basketball court that few his height could ever do. He was declaring for the NBA draft, and this time there was no chance of him withdrawing his name from the list of early entrants.

Chapter 5: With the Fourth Pick of the 2015 NBA Draft

Everyone knew that Kristaps Porzingis was going high in the lottery in 2015. It wasn't expected that he would go first overall, as that was supposed to be a battle between Jahlil Okafor and Karl-Anthony Towns, although Minnesota which had pick number 1 did like the Latvian star. Some draft experts had him going closer to pick number 10, but most had him in the range of picks 3 to 5.

The Philadelphia 76ers were a team doing a harsh rebuild, or a huge tanking job for picks, and reportedly were a team that Kristaps and everyone else didn't want to go to. They had pick number 3. Going into the draft, everyone thought the 76ers would not target a center prospect as that was what they had already done the previous two drafts. But the 76ers had their infamous rebuilding "process" and nobody was sure how they would approach the draft.

The New York Knicks and Phil Jackson had pick number 4. This was where Porzingis wanted to land. The Knicks needed a star prospect, but their fans were not sure about going to Europe for one as they remembered when a pick was thrown away because it was used on Frederic Weis. They also had a big need for a guard.

The Orlando Magic had pick number 5, and as they had wanted him possibly more than anyone the previous year it was likely Porzingis would not go past their pick. While they had good young players at all three frontcourt spots, Porzingis would have still been a good fit, as many believed he could play any of those positions.

Those who Porzingis hired to guide him during the draft process did their job. They kept him away from teams he didn't want, got him exposure to those he had an interest in and also made sure his pre-draft hype matched that of other potential draftees. When they released his measurements, it solidified his spot on some draft boards and moved him way up for other teams.

His numbers were 7-1.25 without shoes, with a 7-6 wingspan and a weight of 230 pounds. Teams were thinking he was 7-0 or 7-1, but when his shoes were added to the equation, and they had to be because nobody played in the NBA without shoes, he was now 7-3. At the combine, Frank Kaminsky and Willie Cauley-Stein just passed the seven foot mark, with shoes. Okafor and

Towns didn't get measured at the combine, but the NBA would list Okafor at 6-11 and 270 pounds with Towns at 7-0 and 250 pounds. On the same list, the NBA originally had Porzingis at 7-0 and 220.

When the draft started, it went to plan, for the first choice. Minnesota went with center Karl-Anthony Towns, KAT. His combination of height and skill, plus his character and his big season at Kentucky, made him the first choice. The Lakers were next, Jahlil Okafor was expected to be their choice, although some rumors had Kristaps Porzingis as the player they wanted.

Pick number 2 by the Lakers was guard D'Angelo Russell. This put a lot of plans other teams had into chaos. The 76ers already had centers Joel Embiid and Nerlens Noel and their major need was at guard, or at least a forward with outside shooting ability. Porzingis may have thought he was going to be pick number 3, but Sam Hinkie and the 76ers always had a plan and they stuck to it once more. Their BPA, best player available, for their draft rankings was center Okafor so they selected him. Most players are disappointed when their name is not called at the draft, but Porzingis was relieved.

He had been telling everyone who interviewed him before the draft that it was his "dream" to be a Knick, but there was still the chance there would be a trade or they would pick another prospect. Point guard Emmanuel Mudiay was still available. Swingman Justise Winslow from Duke was also a player some thought the Knicks might choose. There were also many teams, including Boston with a lot of future picks to offer, who wanted to trade for the Knicks' pick so they could take Winslow. Porzingis, wearing a maroon suit, waited with everyone else for the announcement.

"With the fourth pick in the 2015 NBA Draft, the New York Knicks select, Kristaps Porzingis, from Liepaja, Latvia. He last played for Sevilla, in Spain."

For some, the pick was a shock. Phil Jackson wasn't expected to gamble on an international player. Many thought he would play it safe, and take someone from the college system. When NBA Commissioner Silver announced the pick, many NBA analysts and reporters lined up to say the Knicks made a mistake. ESPN had a statistic lined up, right after the Porzingis pick was made, showing how Nowitzki and Pau Gasol were the only two Europeans to be picked in the lottery and become All-Stars. The days after the draft were filled with news articles about why Porzingis was the wrong choice and destined to be a bust.

The announcement that Porzingis was a Knick was met by crying, yelling and booing by the Knicks fans at the draft. There were melodramatics that would have been more at home on a Jerry Springer show or at a daycare center. The camera zoomed in on a spoiled brat in the audience crying and making a scene, and also plenty of older New York Knicks fans who were giving a thumbs down sign to the pick or holding their head in their hands. It was entertaining viewing for fans of other teams, and a reason why people watch the five hours of the draft. Porzingis didn't care, he was told to expect that reaction and if anything he used it as motivation to show those people they were wrong.

In a small move later in the draft, Phil Jackson found a way to bring in a player that Porzingis was familiar with. He wouldn't join the Knicks as a rookie, but acquiring the draft rights to Spain's Willy Hernangomez was seen as a win for the Knicks. The forward/center was acquired for a couple of future second rounders, after the 76ers chose him at pick 35. Willy had played with and against Kristaps in the Spanish leagues.

It was a quality draft for the Knicks. Two tall players with skill plus a tall point guard who arrived in trade. Porzingis, Jerian Grant and Hernangomez may not have all been expected to be instant stars but were all expected to have good futures in the NBA. There were many positive reviews, as newspapers and Internet sites graded Phil Jackson's draft haul. Matt Moore of CBS gave the Knicks an A, NBADraft.Net gave out a B as did Scott

Gleeson of *USA Today*, while at Yahoo! it was A+ from Kelly Dwyer and B+ from Marc Spears.

There were plenty of critics, and they made a lot of noise so everyone could hear them. They gave their opinion, but the play of Porzingis when he hit the NBA court has now silenced them. The loudest, as was often the case, was Stephen A. Smith. "New York Knick fans were at the Barclays Center booing because we recognize that we have been hoodwinked, bamboozled, led astray, run amuck, and flat out deceived by Phil Jackson and the New York Knicks." George Willis of the *New York Post* had a story about all the boos and added his own thought about Porzingis, "At 233 pounds, Porzingis is as thin as a lamppost and may struggle early with the physical play in the NBA. The reality is since Yao Ming was drafted in 2002, 19 international players have been selected in the NBA lottery and none has been named an All-Star."

The day after the draft, New York sports fans got to see Kristaps in action. It wasn't on the basketball court, it was on the mound before a baseball game. Porzingis threw out the ceremonial first pitch at a New York Mets game. His brother, Martins, pointed out the obvious, "Nobody plays baseball in Latvia." Mets pitcher Jon Niese shook Kristaps' hand and said, "That's the tallest guy I've ever seen in my life." Both Kristaps Porzingis and Jerian Grant got their pitches to home plate on the full, a great accomplishment for the Latvian as it was the first time he had been on a baseball field.

For around 48 hours after the draft, there was plenty of conjecture about whether Carmelo Anthony liked the choice or he disliked it. It all started when Carmelo let loose a strange tweet after Porzingis had been selected. "What's understood doesn't need to be spoken upon #DestiNY #TheFutureIsNow."

The perception was that Anthony wanted someone who could help right away, and plenty of reporters quoted anonymous sources saying that Carmelo was displeased or even furious with the Knicks and Phil Jackson. If that actually was the case, there wasn't really a player who was really ready to play NBA that was expected to go at pick 4, although trading the pick for a veteran would have helped the Knicks if the future really was to be now. Emmanuel Mudiay was the other prospect many expected the Knicks to draft, he didn't go to college and played only a few games in China before an injury stopped his season and he was less ready than Porzingis. After a few days, Carmelo said nice things about the choice and nobody mentioned it again.

Phil Jackson has said that Carmelo watched a pre-draft Porzingis workout so he should have been familiar with his ability. Porzingis put any of Melo's fears to rest by showing him how he played, and also talking about his childhood hairstyle. Kristaps told Carmelo how his cornrows hairstyle was inspired by him and Allen Iverson, when they played for Denver. Anthony told *Sports Illustrated*, "After that I was like, 'All right, O.K., I'm riding with you from now on.' The kid has an aura about him."

Four Summer League games gave fans a brief glimpse of what Porzingis could do. But they were games against few NBA players, as the rosters were mostly filled with free agents with little or no NBA experience. He averaged 10.5 points a game on 48% shooting. Porzingis wore number 46 in these games. One important game was against the 76ers, and Jahlil Okafor. Porzingis had 9 points and 3 blocks; Okafor had 18 points on 18 shots but no blocks. Porzingis was more efficient, shooting 3 of 5 from the field although he did commit 7 fouls.

When the pre-season started, nobody knew exactly who would be starting next to Carmelo for the Knicks. Coach Derek Fisher had a few names to consider. Porzingis was at the top of his list, to be the starting power forward, but other players also had a shot to start next to Carmelo and free agent acquisition center Robin Lopez.

Derrick Williams made a lot of sense, a former number 2 draft choice, he still had potential and with a similar size to Carmelo maybe they could work well as combo-forwards. Kyle O'Quinn and Kevin Seraphin were taller options than Williams, and would have added more rebounding. A smaller lineup was also possible, with Carmelo at power forward and someone like Cleanthony Early at small forward. The six pre-season games the Knicks had would help Coach Fisher decide.

In the first pre-season game, against a team from Brazil, Porzingis had 7 points in 21 minutes. Porzingis' first time on the court against real NBA players would be the next pre-season game, the Washington Wizards. The Knicks won, Williams led the team in points and O'Quinn led the Knicks in rebounds. Porzingis had a solid 9 points on 9 shots, with 2 blocks. Derrick Williams would continue to lead the team in scoring for a few more games, which didn't hurt his chances of getting the starting spot ahead of Porzingis for the regular season.

The idea was to start lottery selection Porzingis ahead of the free agent journeymen the Knicks had picked up during the offseason, but he hadn't pushed ahead of the challengers during the pre-season games. The last pre-season game was against the Celtics, and Coach Fisher may have seen some things he liked from Porzingis. Kristaps was using his height and skills to do things the other power forwards could not. He led the Knicks in assists that game, with 4. For a team with Anthony at forward shooting a lot, to have the other forward able to pass the ball well was a plus. Kristaps also brought in 3 offensive rebounds, showing that while he wasn't as strong as others he could still hit the offensive glass.

Not many rookies get to start their first ever NBA game, but Kristaps Porzingis had grabbed that opportunity. While many people would question a lot of the moves Derek Fisher was going to make, his choice to go with the tall rookie at power forward was one many agreed with.

Chapter 6: Becoming a New York Hero in 10 Games

"A lot of fans weren't happy that they drafted me, but I have to do everything that's in my hands to turn those booing fans into clapping fans. There's nothing I can do. I was happy about it. I want to be a part of this organization. I know the fans are a little harsh sometimes, but that's how it is here in New York and I'm ready for it."

Kristaps Porzingis had a message for Knicks fans on draft night but he would have to wait a few months to get the chance to turn them into clapping fans. When the season started, it took him a few plays to make some fans in Madison Square Garden stand up and applaud, a couple of games for others, and a few weeks into the season there wasn't any Knick fan who was saying he didn't want Phil Jackson to have drafted Porzingis. Something else happened, which showed how much popularity he had, a Porzingis jersey became the must-have item for sports fans in NYC as well as around the NBA and the world.

His first game was on October 28, 2014 in Milwaukee, Wisconsin. Porzingis started and the Knicks had a huge win over the Bucks, 122 to 97. 18,717 people in Wisconsin can say they saw Porzingis play his first NBA game, although it is likely that many of the locals left early as their team had a big loss.

Against the Bucks, Porzingis played 24 minutes. His first basket in the NBA was when he caught the ball in the corner, drove and stopped just short of the paint, and then shot the ball off the glass for two. In the second half he hit a straight-on three-pointer, the first of many long-range bombs in his rookie season. It was 16 points on 11 shots, a good result although he did struggle from the field. He went 3 for 11 from the field, but his 9 of 12 on free throws helped balance out his game. Derrick Williams led the Knicks with 24 points.

The home opener for the Knicks at Madison Square Garden in New York, New York was against the Atlanta Hawks and their four All-Stars. Jeff Teague, Al Horford, Kyle Korver and Paul Millsap were too good for Kristaps and his Knicks. Atlanta won, 112 to 101. Carmelo led the Knicks in scoring, with 25, but Porzingis had the best +/- rating of the New York starters.

While -5 isn't the best result for his time on the court, all the other starters for his team had a negative in double-figures so Porzingis did have a solid game compared to them. His 3 steals, 1 block and 6 defensive rebounds showed how he can be a force when the other team has the ball. He scored 10 points on 10 shots, and missed all 4 attempts from downtown.

They started the season with a road win and a home loss, and followed that with a road win at the Wizards. The Knicks didn't need anything magical from Porzingis, Carmelo Anthony took down Washington by scoring 37 points. Porzingis was efficient in the 117 to 110 win, he hit 3 of 6 field goals and 2 of 2 free throws.

While he was getting noticed in his first three NBA games, it was his fourth game that made people really pay attention. It was his first double-double, and while the Knicks lost they did keep it close against the San Antonio Spurs and also had the lead after the first quarter. Tim Duncan set a record by winning his 954th NBA game and after the game told everyone about Porzingis, "He was impressive. He is a young guy, but his skill set is there."

The highlight of the game was when Carmelo missed a shot, and Porzingis flew over the San Antonio defenders to rebound the ball with one hand and dunk it down for two points. The lowlight was Porzingis falling to the court, along with two Spurs, and then Carmelo landed on his teammate. Kristaps had 13 points, 14 rebounds, 3 steals and 2 blocks. The Spurs won, 94 to 84, but the NBA was now aware that Porzingis was a great rookie.

It wasn't the easiest schedule for the Knicks, but it certainly was something that got Porzingis TV time, his next game was against the Cleveland Cavaliers and LeBron James. Porzingis went against All-Star power forward Kevin Love, and beat him. The score after the first quarter was Knicks 32 and Cavs 18. That didn't last, Cleveland won 96 to 86. Carmelo lost his position battle; he had 17 points on 18 shots while LeBron had 23 points on 23 shots.

Kevin Love brought in 11 points and 12 rebounds. He needed to take 13 shots though, and he only hit 4 of them. He didn't record a block or steal. Porzingis dominated on both ends of the court. He had 13 points on 6 of 11 shooting with 4 rebounds 2 steals and 2 blocks. Two of Porzingis' points came on a putback dunk over Love, as he flew up and over and with one hand grabbed the ball and flushed it.

The sixth game of the season for New York was a repeat from earlier, the Milwaukee Bucks. Fans wanted to know which team had the top super athlete. Giannis Antetokounmpo had missed the first game due to suspension, and like Porzingis he was young and long, and also still growing. They both also had names that were hard to spell, which was why fans considered it to be "Greek Freak" going against "Zinger."

Porzingis was great against the Bucks, with another double-double, but thanks to a very unexpected 22 points off the bench from John Henson, the Bucks won the game, 99 to 92. Antetokounmpo had 20 points. Once again, Porzingis had a putback dunk, which was one of the best plays of the game. Porzingis had 14 points, 13 rebounds, a block and an apology. "There's little things that I didn't do well to help us finish the game well. I was expecting a better game from myself. I take a lot of responsibility for what happened." He was a rookie, he shot 6 of 13, he wasn't the worst player out there. Calderon started and was scoreless, Sasha Vujacic started and went 1 for 5, Carmelo shot 6 of 16 and Derrick Williams went 4 for 11 off the bench.

Everyone in MSG was expecting a huge game from Kobe Bryant when the Lakers came to town. Instead of that they got a win, thanks to their dominating frontcourt and a double-double from the tall rookie. Porzingis had 12 points, 10 rebounds and 2 blocks. He also led all players in +/- with +18. Carmelo had 24 points, while shooting 8 for 20. Kobe had 18 points, and shot poorly with 6 for 19. The Knicks won, 99 to 95. Coach Fisher was ejected by the referees. They said Porzingis fouled Bryant on a three-pointer, Fisher disagreed, and the referees sent him away.

The eighth game of the season saw the Knicks return to a .500 record as they defeated a Toronto Raptors team that had an All-Star backcourt. Porzingis and the Knicks went north across the border for their fourth win of the 2015-16 season. With point guard Kyle Lowry and shooting guard DeMar DeRozan combining for 52 points it was a shock loss for Toronto, with the Knicks winning 111 to 109. Porzingis had only 8 points but the Knicks had bench production with 17 points from Lance Thomas and 15 from Langston Galloway. The highlight, yet again, was a Porzingis putback. This time he jumped over four players, grabbed the ball with two hands and dunked it, to the delight of the Knicks players on the bench.

There was no Knick fan booing Kristaps now. If he had any doubters, their next game shut them down. Something that makes fans cheer a player is late-game heroics. Porzingis seemed to win the game at Charlotte by hitting a three-pointer as time expired. There were 0.6 seconds on the clock, he caught the ball and shot, and it went in. But the referees watched the video replays, his fingers may have still been on the ball as time expired, it was very close but the decision went to the home team and the Charlotte Hornets won with the basket being disallowed. That a rookie was not only on the floor in clutch time but had a play run for him shows how highly the Knicks thought of Porzingis.

The Knicks had no reason to exclude Porzingis from the last second of play; he had played a great game. 5 of 10 shooting for 10 points, 15 rebounds, 2 blocks and a +/- of +9. Carmelo had a good game too, 29 points on 12 of 25 shooting. There was no unofficial name for all the Porzingis publicity, but this game reminded Knicks fans of something similar from the past. "Linsanity" was several years before when Jeremy Lin brought excitement back to MSG. At this game at Time Warner Cable Arena in Charlotte, he played a huge part off the bench with 17 points on 7 of 11 shooting. The next time the Knicks played the Hornets, the show was only Porzingis.

Outplaying Kevin Love twice in the first few weeks of his career, Porzingis did just that. The Knicks lost to the Cavs once again, but Porzingis won his battle at power forward. Cleveland would go on to win their first NBA championship that season but they couldn't contain Kristaps. Love shot 2 of 10, Porzingis shot 5 of 11, the best power forward was Porzingis as Cleveland's Tristan Thompson only went 1 for 4 off the bench as well. Porzingis had 11 points and 7 rebounds. LeBron was too much though; his 31 points got the Cavs the win, 90 to 84. Like the rest of the NBA, Love struggled to stop the combination of length and agility that Porzingis possesses. Love isn't small, at 6-10, but he looks it when Porzingis at 7-3 is next to him. It had been an amazing start to Porzingis' rookie season.

The headlines that followed the draft were soon forgotten by the newspapers as they instead embraced the Porzingis phenomenon. In November, some of the news headlines were "The hype is real: Kristaps Porzingis is the hero the Knicks need," "Knicks' Porzingis Takes New York and the NBA By Storm" and "Kristaps Porzingis is blowing away the NBA world."

Kristaps was blowing away all the NBA rookies too, especially the ones in the East. For October and November, he was named the Eastern Conference Rookie of the Month. Karl-Anthony Towns got the award for the West. KAT won the award for his conference every month of the season while Porzingis got the East's award for the next two months as well, and was considered for the award later in the season too. The other winners in the East that season were Myles Turner, Josh Richardson and Norman Powell.

It wasn't all Kristaps, it is a family business. Everyone is in New York with him, making sure that basketball was the only thing he had to concern himself with. Janis is his agent, as is Andy Miller who has many NBA clients like Kevin Garnett, Timofey Mozgov and Willy Hernangomez. Martins is Kristaps' manager. His mother cooks for Kristaps, helping him stay healthy and add bulk, while his father studies every game and every play and gives his son advice. His brothers also accompany Kristaps in a sort of bodyguard role.

Porzingis and the Knicks were about to start talking about the playoffs. After a solid start to the season, they put together a win streak. The four-game win streak would include Porzingis setting his season-high for points as well as the Knicks defeating one of the powerhouse NBA teams, at their venue.

Chapter 7: His Amazing NBA Rookie Season

Sometimes teams figure out a rookie quickly, or they hit the proverbial "rookie wall," but that didn't happen to Kristaps. The rest of his rookie year was full of highlights and super statistics.

On November 17 when the Charlotte Hornets visited New York, the Knicks played Porzingis 31 minutes and he produced 29 points. 2 of 2 from long range, 7 of 7 on free throws, they were numbers that only someone like Stephen Curry was expected to produce but 7-3 Porzingis had that result against the Hornets. Porzingis is a foot taller than Curry, but what they have in common are uncommon skills and also that they sell tickets and gets fans watching the games more than most other players.

When Porzingis and the Knicks beat the Rockets, the Latvian did something that no rookie had done since Tim Duncan in 1998. He had 24 points, 14 rebounds and seven blocks. A day before that, Porzingis and the Knicks defeated Oklahoma City, by 3 points, in OKC.

His rookie season success also led to endorsement deals, which not only brought in some money but some useful items for him and his family. He signed with a mattress company, and Porzingis received a custom-made, oversized bed in that deal. Promoting Delta Air Lines got him plane tickets to Latvia whenever he needed them.

In early December, the Knicks beat the 76ers and Philadelphia fans would have been thinking they drafted the wrong player. Jahlil Okafor didn't play as he was expected. Kristaps Porzingis certainly did play; he played very well with 17 points, 10 rebounds and 4 blocks. The 76ers fans would have been wishing the 7-3 Latvian was on their team, Porzingis shot 6 of 10 from the field and was 2 of 2 on threes. Around the time the calendar went from 2015 to 2016, the Knicks had a run of 6 wins in 7 games. Porzingis' biggest game during that time was against the Celtics; he had 26 points and 0 turnovers.

On January 16, 2016 *Newsday* had a headline, "Knicks' Kristaps Porzingis No. 4 in NBA jersey sales." The official results from the NBA were Stephen Curry, LeBron James and Kobe Bryant as the three most popular and the New York rookie close behind. Porzingis wears size 16 shoes. He started his NBA career wearing Nike

Kobe X Elite shoes, and with a marker he would color parts of them to comply with NBA rules.

Porzingis was used to some coaching turmoil, previously in Spain, but maybe he and others didn't expect the Knicks to fire Derek Fisher on February 8. One former Laker was out as the coach, and former Laker Kurt Rambis took over on an interim, but possibly permanent, basis as head coach. It didn't impact Porzingis, he still got lots of playing time and plenty of shots.

In February, Porzingis was part of All-Star Weekend when he competed in the 2016 NBA Rising Stars Game. There wasn't a lot of competition, little defense was played as Team USA defeated Team World, 157 to 154. Porzingis was the top scorer with 30 points. Emmanuel Mudiay and Zach LaVine also scored 30 points, Andrew Wiggins had 29.

The two teams only had 4 blocks combined in the game, but Kristaps got one of them. The scoring showcase did show all the skills Porzingis has with the ball. He shot 5 of 8 on three-pointers, a percentage of 62.5%. He passed for 4 assists, which wasn't difficult with such a high score as his team had 45 assists. 12 of 16 from the field in 28 minutes of play, he had a big game in what won't be his last appearance at the All-Star break festivities.

Porzingis didn't struggle with his new team, league or country during his rookie season. With English skills far above most other draftees from countries where English is not the primary language, he was ready for all aspects of the NBA and everyday life. He also found a restaurant he liked, the Cheesecake Factory. Porzingis is very happy in NYC, "I love it here. New York's the place to be."

As the season progressed, Porzingis kept on producing. In an away game against the Clippers, he led his team in scoring with 23 points. At Washington a week later, he had 20 points and 3 blocks. On March 23 he had what might have been his best game of the season. Porzingis may have grown up wanting to play like Pau Gasol, and in this game he outplayed him. The Knicks won, and they kept Gasol to 4 points on 2 of 7 shooting. Porzingis matched his season-high, and therefore career-high, of 29 points. Kristaps shot 11 of 16 from the field, hitting 3 of 6 three-pointers.

It didn't take long for Porzingis to acquire a lot of nicknames. Zinger was one that many used, but Porzingis said he was not a fan of it. It had been given to him in Spain by one of his coaches. "He started calling me Zinger and it was just like, yeah. He was a good coach and I liked him but that nickname, at that moment, I didn't like it that much." KP or KP6, Porzingis liked them but fans didn't. Other names associated with him have included Unicorn, Godzingis and Porzingod. Kevin

Durant is a fan of Porzingis, "He can shoot, he can make the right plays, he can defend, he's a 7-footer that can shoot all the way out to the 3-point line. That's rare, and block shots, that's like a unicorn in this league."

Playing all 82 games may have been a goal of his when the season started, but he fell a bit short of that and his season also ended early. He didn't want it to, and he told the *New York Post*, "I'm young, and I always want to be on the floor. At the same time, I want to be smart about this. Nothing really to gain in the last few games but I think I'll be back for the last two, three games hopefully. But it's not my decision at the end of the day."

Porzingis missed the last seven games of the season due to a shoulder injury. They were out of the playoff race, and didn't have a draft pick to worry about, so making sure Porzingis was in perfect health for 2016-17 was the priority for the New York Knicks. They shut him down, eliminating any risk of him causing a greater injury to his shoulder by playing in a few meaningless games.

He had missed three other games during the season. An upper respiratory illness was the reason Porzingis missed a game in late January. He missed a home game against the Pistons in early March when a bruised lower left leg injury saw him ruled out just before the game started. The only other game he missed during his rookie season was on March 13 at the L.A. Lakers. Porzingis was hit by a sudden stomach virus and couldn't play. In the final seconds of the game, it was tied before Jose Calderon hit the winning three-pointer.

During his rookie season he reached heights few thought he could get, like being a starter for every game he played in his rookie campaign and putting up a very good set of statistics, but just being that tall and effective was an achievement. There have only been a small number of players who were taller than Porzingis and appeared in an NBA game, and few had his skills.

Less than twenty players who were 7-4 in height or taller have played in the NBA. Among those giants who had the rare ability to look down on Porzingis, only Rik Smits, Yao Ming and Ralph Sampson had skills similar to Porzingis. None had the range of the Latvian, and only Sampson could play power forward while the others were strictly centers. It is rare for any rookie to hit better than 80% on free throws, Porzingis did that. He even had the best foul shot percentage of any rookie who measured in at 7-1 or taller, who played more than a handful of minutes. Even 7-0 rookie Dirk Nowitzki only shot 77.3%. In 2015-16, rookie Porzingis shot 83.8% on foul shots. Yao was 81.1% for his first season.

Only Yao and Arvydas Sabonis had NBA seasons better at the free throw line than Porzingis, for players 7-3 in height or taller. Tibor Pleiss could be added to the list, but his 2 for 2 total foul shots in a season isn't really a large enough sample size. There is another list that Porzingis shares with 7-3 Lithuanian center Sabonis, and that is players in NBA history 7-3 or taller who hit at least 10 threes while shooting at least 30% from long range. Manute Bol did that one time, Zydrunas Ilgauskas did it twice, and Sabonis also did it for two seasons with a high of 49 threes made. Porzingis hit 81 three-pointers as a rookie, while Sabonis was over 30 years of age when he did it.

For PER, player efficiency rating, Porzingis was at 81 in the NBA. His PER was 17.7. Carmelo was the only Knick ranked above him, at 41 in the NBA with a 20.3 PER. This is for counting Knicks who played more than a few minutes, as Thanasis Antetokounmpo actually led the NBA in PER but with only 6 minutes for the entire season he doesn't qualify for league-leader categories. Porzingis was ranked ahead of many players and some of the big names were Ricky Rubio, Jahlil Okafor, Aaron Gordon, Tim Duncan, Rajon Rondo, Andrew Wiggins, Andrew Bogut and Serge Ibaka.

The New York Knicks have made Porzingis the cornerstone of the franchise. In only one year, Phil Jackson has brought in and sent out a plethora of players as he looks for those who fit with Porzingis, and Carmelo. He signed shooter Jimmer Fredette and combo-guard Tony Wroten late in Porzingis' rookie season.

After the season, the Knicks really shook things up. First was a new coach, the third of Porzingis' short NBA career, Jeff Hornacek. Then Porzingis got to see what a blockbuster trade was all about, as the Knicks sent out Jose Calderon, Jerian Grant and Robin Lopez and received Derrick Rose.

Kristaps Porzingis is unlike any NBA player. There are no players in the NBA with his combination of amazing height, agility and skills. He also came to the NBA from a small country where basketball was not huge, although it now is because of Porzingis. A backyard basketball court in Latvia to Madison Square Garden, Porzingis made a dream become a reality.

About the Author

Benjamin Southerland is a lifelong Chicagoland resident. Southerland developed a strong interest for politics and government during his college years through his study of leaders who have shaped history, such as Winston Churchill, Napoleon, and Thomas Jefferson. Southerland is also interested in individuals who have impacted the world of sports and entertainment. He has studied and written about politicians, world leaders, athletes, and celebrities. He researches these fascinating figures extensively in order to determine what has shaped their worldviews and contributed to their success. He aims for his books to give readers a deep understanding of the achievements, inspirations, and goals of the world's most influential individuals. Follow Benjamin Southerland at his website benjaminsoutherland.com to learn about his latest books.

Made in the USA
Coppell, TX
30 May 2020